The "Fix-it" Box

Jacob Noel

TO MY BEST FRIEND AND BEAUTIFUL
WIFE AMANDA

You make this wondrous adventure of life so
special. I am ever grateful for your friendship,
support, and steadfast love.

CONTENTS

Author's Note

I am beginning the endeavor of writing this book without the slightest clue of whether or not it will be read by anyone, or if it will even be completed in the near future. I have to smile at my own unsure stance, but I am excited about the chance to share what the Lord has shown me over the years. This work is really the compilation of many sermons and messages that I have been honored to preach and share. In all honesty, I can say that the teachings found in this book come from the study of the greatest book, The Bible. Some of the worthwhile lessons are those that I learned along my journey from the many great mentors that have been placed in my life. I am grateful to have been able to learn from so many incredible examples of faith. Without such examples, I most certainly would not be who I am today. Thank you for your teaching, patience, and steadfast stance for righteousness.

This book was written in order to encourage those who need encouraging, to empower those who feel weak, and to remind us all of who we truly are in Jesus Christ. Any and all proceeds from this work will go towards furthering medical missions. My wife and I are medical missionaries (currently serving with Healthcare Ministries and attending LSU School of Medicine). All proceeds will be placed in a special fund for paying off any medical school debt (that would keep us from full-time mission work) or towards supporting full-time medical missions once we are on the field.

I pray that this book empowers you to live out the calling that the Lord has placed upon your life. Enjoy the incredible journey to finding identity in the Father.

Blessings,

Jacob Noel

Introduction:

Identity Found...

The sound of a garage door opening creaked through the side entrance door to my home. Being a strapping lad of nine, I instantly scoured the front corridor for the most inconspicuous and stealthy hiding places available. I knew I only had moments before the daily routine of my father's return from work began. Thinking quickly, I lurked into the shadowy cover of our guest bathroom. Moments later, I heard the doorknob turn as my father gingerly entered the foyer, possibly aware of my presence. I could hardly breathe for fear that I would be discovered at an inopportune time. Then, when the moment was right, I leapt from my cover, certain of victory, and let out a shout that would reverberate throughout the neighborhood.

"Ahhhhhh! Got ya Pop!" I shrieked.

Definitively startled, but certainly not surprised, my father jumped! Then, after the shock of being scared half to death had subsided, laughter erupted and an impromptu wrestling match began. Of course I was pinned quickly, but the fun was overwhelming. As the laughter died down, my mother entered the room and gave my "Pop" a long, loving hug and quick kiss to say hello.

I have always cherished my memories of our daily welcoming routine after my father returned from work. My brother and I grew up in a wonderful family. My father and mother have been rock-solid examples of Christ's love for my brother and me for as long as I can remember. Everyday, I was confident that we would share life together. In my home environment, I was taught to feel secure, whole, and deeply loved. Never did I have to wonder about my parent's feelings towards me or towards one another. I was totally accepted, totally loved, and if I ever failed to live up to my parent's rules, I was sure that I was totally forgiven. These principles, based on scripture, formed the foundation of my understanding of my identity in Christ.

Identity Lost...

I will never forget the moment that I saw him, a young boy of scarcely fourteen years who had completely lost his understanding of his true identity. Looking into his eyes, I saw complete and total emptiness. His face, covered with tattooed emblems, symbolized his stature as a life-long member of a notorious Salvadoran street gang.

The prison doors slid shut and were locked into

position behind me as I stood in the courtyard of the high-security prison for youth gang members. As a King's Castle Ministries missionary, I was accustomed to working on the hardened streets of San Salvador, but I had never been in a place like this before. Hundreds of "youth," most seemed to be merely children, milled about the prison, each bearing the tattooed markings of heinous crimes and senseless acts of violence.

Realizing that this may be the only opportunity to share with these children about the love of Christ, I swallowed hard and said a quick prayer. I was fearful that my limited Spanish would evoke laughter and sneers from the hardened young men. However, I was amazed. As I began to share of the hope that Christ gives us to overcome our failures, I began to see a glimmer of hope in the previously grim countenances of the boys.

These young men had lost their true identity. Surely they are defined by society as rebels, gangsters, murderers, thieves, and villains. To be sure, these titles are well-deserved, but I am confident that this is not who God intended them to be. Somewhere along the line these men believed a lie that they were without true identity. Searching desperately for acceptance, family, respect, and purpose, they traded away their divinely inspired identity for a shadow of falsehood.

Whether young children desiring a parent's embrace, teenagers looking for a social support group, or Wall Street businessmen striving to achieve elusive contracts, all of humanity longs for acceptance, love, and security. In essence, we want to know, "Who am I? Where do I fit? and Where am I loved?"

The answer to all three of the above questions is

immersed in knowing Christ. His Love knows no bounds, His faithfulness is never-ending, and His forgiveness is unlimited. Whether you have followed Christ for many years, or are not even sure about His existence, I pray that this book will be an inspiration to you, allowing you the opportunity to ponder the questions in life that deserve pondering. I pray that through reading this book, you will experience the love of Christ, and ultimately understand that His love is more powerful than your past, more complete than you could imagine, and overall, simply life changing.

Section One:

[The "Fix-it" Box]

From 1982 until 1994, the Hasbro toy company produced one of the most prolific and, in my opinion, one of the most enduring lines of toys. "The G.I. Joe: A Real American Hero" line of action figures was by far the most treasured of all of my earthly possessions from the ages of five until about eleven. For those of you thinking of the twelve-inch version of the G.I. Joe, I assure you; this was not the "doll for boys," flashing through your mind. I am referring to the plastic molded three and three-quarter-inch action figurines, with accompanying blasters and battle-ready accessories.

Each action figure held a world of adventure limited only by my vast imagination. Each Christmas morning or birthday party assuredly included at least one of the prized figurines. Interestingly, each action figure was held together via plastic molding, a screw, and also a small black rubber band that allowed for great flexibility in the midst of heated battles.

A few rather astute children may have noticed that when the torso of the G.I. Joe figurine was twisted repeatedly, the toy would spin to life in a tornado-twisting attack pattern while the rubber band recoiled and untwisted. However this incredible maneuver could lead to undesired consequences as the rubber band aged or was stretched beyond its capacity.

One such day, I was engaged in a raid against Cobra Commander and G.I. Joe's worst enemies. In the midst of the battle, the dreaded helicopter-punch attack resulted in one of my G.I.'s literally breaking into pieces. My six-year-old heart was crushed, as I sat in my room with only the pieces of what had once been the mighty warrior named "Muskrat."

Thinking quickly, I ran to my Papa's office. There, I glanced at the closet door. I knew what would be on the top shelf. There would be a stack of McDermott Automatic Welding hats, a pack or two of yellow manila folders, and most importantly, the "Fix-it" box.

"Pop," I cried, "Can you fix him?"

My Father stopped working at his desk, came over to me, and gingerly took the pieces from my hands. He smiled compassionately and said, "Let's put him in the 'Fix-it' box." I agreed. I knew that if anyone could repair the damage to "Muskrat" and get him back into fighting shape, it was my father.

I don't know exactly when my Pop began using the "Fix-it" box, but the small worn shoebox served as the first-aid and level-one trauma center for my brother's and my toys for years. Though I knew that some "injuries" were too grave to repair, I felt such peace knowing that my Pop was going to look into each case and do his best to fix my toys.

Often, as was the case with "Muskrat" some time later, they would appear back in action as my Father, an engineer, took time to repair the damage.

Now, as an adult, I look back at this work with incredible fondness. My father was often busy with hectic schedules and difficult engineering problems, but I never felt that he was too busy for the things that bothered me.

What a picture of what our Heavenly Father does for each one of us.

Misconception

In the world today, I am convinced that there are many misconceptions about Jesus Christ. Specifically, there is the idea that God is angry at humans. It is true that God is just, righteous, and hates sin; however, there is no indication whatsoever that He is angry at humanity. In fact, throughout scripture, we see quite the opposite sentiment expressed.

In the Gospel of Matthew, the author describes Jesus' fulfillment of a prophesy in the book of Isaiah that clearly expresses the personality of Jesus the Messiah.

"He will not crush the weakest reed or put out a flickering candle." - Matthew 12:20; Isaiah 42:3 (NIV)

This is an incredible insight into God's character! It completely reverses the idea that God would be angry, unloving, and slow to forgiveness. What does this strange-sounding verse mean?

A bruised reed or a smoldering flame is indicative or the frailness of our own moral standing in front of a righteous God. This beautiful verse explains that God has the heart and identity of one who sees brokenness and nurtures it back to health. Where we are unable to help ourselves and make mistake after mistake, Christ sees a broken reed, but *He never loses hope*.

What does God do with the countless people (myself often included) that seem to be broken reeds or smoldering flames? He has a heart to restore them. In essence, He desires to place them in His "Fix-it" box.

Interestingly enough, when Christ moves in our lives and begins to mend broken reeds and restore the passion and hope of a smoldering wick, He does not stop at only repairing the damage. Christ goes far beyond reparation. He adopts us into His family as sons and daughters! Where we see failure, He sees love. Where we see impossible resolution, Christ desires divine intervention and indiscriminate, unabashed, selfless love.

The natural tendency of humanity is to demand retribution for past mistakes. The truth is that for most people, forgiveness doesn't make much sense. We want justice. We innately desire that those who hurt us must be punished. On the contrary, God has quite a different plan for "fixing" those who have been bruised, even of their own accord. He desires sonship. When our lives return from the "Fix-it" box of Christ, not only are we no longer broken, but incredibly, we are also adopted and accepted into

His loving arms as His children.

A Father's Love

14 For as many as are led by the Spirit of God, these are sons of God. 15 For you did not receive the spirit of bondage again to fear, but you received the Spirit of adoption by whom we cry out, "Abba, Father." 16 The Spirit Himself bears witness with our spirit that we are children of God, 17 and if children, then heirs—heirs of God and joint heirs with Christ, if indeed we suffer with *Him,* that we may also be glorified together. – Romans 8:14-17 (NIV)

Vines New Testament Dictionary explains the following about the word Abba in the Bible:

"Abba" is the word framed by the lips of infants, and betokens unreasoning trust; "father" expresses

an intelligent apprehension of the relationship. The two together express the love and intelligent confidence of the child.

When my father would come home each day from work, I rushed into his arms. I did not seek something from him. Rather, I wanted to be near him. I wanted spend time with him. My thoughts did not wander to *my* own desires, *my* own wants, or *my* own needs. My heart was full of joy to be embraced by a father who came home to see me.

My father, who I have always called the French word, Papá, often bent over backwards to do special things for my brother and me. Even though he is a busy engineer, I cannot remember a major event in my life where he was not present. Today, I have no idea how he did this! He never left me wondering if he would come, never broke a promise, and never dealt harshly with my brother, my mother, or me.

As a child, when I would rush into his arms, I did not think of the things he did for me…it was really all about being near him and my mother! I just wanted to be around them!

It is not about me!

I am amazed at how easily my relationship with Christ so often becomes focused on the things that I need, want, or desire. This is often a natural reaction to difficult situations and circumstances. However, when I read the incredible word "Abba" in the New Testament, it shows a clear understanding of the fact that Jesus was expressing that the relationship between a believer and the Father God is not only about our needs, but more so about being *with* the Father. The joy of our lives is not found in meeting our needs or desires. The joy of our hearts and the nourishment of our souls are realized when we are found in Christ. We are whole when we are resting in His powerful arms. When we run to him, abide in Him, and enjoy knowing who Christ is in us, then we find the fullness of joy that is often promised in the scriptures. When we can run and tumble with the love of the Father filling our hearts, minds, spirits and souls, we can then, and only then, understand that knowing Christ is not about us. Knowing "Abba" is truly about knowing the LOVE of the Father!

What a love this is!

I want to encourage you. If you have yet to know this love, do not wait another minute. If you are tired of living without knowing the joy of being wrapped in Christ's loving embrace, do not waste another moment reading this book. Stop now. Enjoy His peace. It will surpass your understanding (Philippians 4:7).

Life without worry

Recently, my Father and I were discussing the old "Fix-it" box. I asked my Father about the box, and with a smile, he said, "Jacob, do you know why I had the 'Fix-it' box? I just didn't want you to worry. You and your brother would come to me with a broken toy, and I just wanted to give you a place to put those things so that you could be at peace again."

I am amazed that though the Gospels are filled with the story of Jesus' life, we have only a few of his actual messages. Often within the narrative of the Gospels, we see only the words, "Jesus taught the people." However, there are times when the writers of the Gospels do record His messages. I am convinced that each time in the scriptures that the teachings of Jesus are actually recorded, we must pay close attention.

One such message is found in Matthew 6:25-35 and also in Luke 12:22-31. In this teaching, Jesus specifically teaches us not to worry! Think about this. Many times, when one thinks of things that are contrary to Jesus' teaching, words like hatred, greed, envy, lust, or jealousy come to mind. We hardly think of worry. However, it is one of the key points in two of the Gospels! As children of Abba Father, we are not created to worry!

There is stark difference between preparation and worry. Preparation is necessary so that we can accomplish what the Lord calls us to do. Imagine trying to do well in school without studying for an exam or trying to cook a fine meal with no ingredients. These things would be impossible. Of course is it necessary to prepare for the things we do in life. However, when we worry, we replace faith with fear. We no longer allow ourselves to bask in the peace of the Father as we lose our grip on the trust that is so vital to the relationship of a child and their parents.

Trust is the Key.

Luke 11:9-13 clearly expresses the Father's love for us. It teaches us to release fear and instead find peace by fully trusting the Father's love.

9 "So I say to you: Ask and it will be given to you; seek and you will find; knock and the door will be opened to you. 10 For everyone who asks receives; the one who seeks finds; and to the one who knocks, the door will be opened.

11 "Which of you fathers, if your son asks for a fish, will give him a snake instead? 12 Or if he asks for an egg, will give him a scorpion? 13 If you then, though you are evil, know how to give good gifts to your children, how much more will

your Father in heaven give the Holy Spirit to those who ask him!" – Luke 11:9-13 (NIV)

One of my favorite scriptures emphasizes the crux of the Biblical explanation of a life against worry. In Proverbs 3:5-6, the Bible reverberates with one of the most comforting, joyous, and yet shocking scriptures ever written.

Trust in the Lord with all of your heart and lean not on your own understanding.   In all your ways acknowledge Him and He shall direct your path. – Proverbs 3:5-6 (NIV)

The wording here is quite interesting to me. There is a substantial difference between *trust* and *belief*. It is very common for people to believe in the Lord. However, the scripture does not say "believe" in the

Lord. The word "trust" is specifically used. Belief is believing that the Lord can do anything. Trust in this sense, is believing that God can do anything *in my situation*. Trust is personalized. Often, it is much easier to believe that God can heal the sick, provide for those in need, or restore the broken hearted. However, when I am worried about a doctor's report, if I am in need, or if I have been hurt, trust is required.

The beauty of trusting in the Lord is that He is not far away. He is not silent when we call to Him. The scriptures affirm that He is quick to hear the prayers of His people. Moreover, as a Father, He is faithful to walk through difficulties with us. Just as I ran to be with my father when he returned from work each day I see in the scriptures, that God the Father loves to love his children. His love is not conditional, changing, or temporary. He is trustworthy and true.

I am sure that even as you read this book, it is possible that you have been hurt or even rejected by religious people in the past. I want to assure you that these religious people, as well-meaning as they may have been, were only religious *people*. They were not Christ. People of all kinds, including zealous and heartfelt Christians, make mistakes. However, God does not make mistakes. His heart is to restore and revive even the faintest hope.

How do we deal with the difficulties of life? What happens when things seem overwhelming, bruised, or smoldering?

We take our issue or problem and place it in the "Fix-it" box of the Heavenly Father.

In Isaiah 55, there is a wonderful promise that Christ fulfills in our lives even today. We can be sure that as we trust in Him, any issue, great or small, is important enough to merit His attention, His love, and His healing power.

Take some time now and spend a few minutes in prayer. If you have not prayed before or have not prayed in a long time, do not worry. Prayer is simply sharing thoughts and words with Christ. If there is any need, any hurt, or any doubt in your heart, place it in the "Fix-it" box of the Father.

"Come, all you who are thirsty, come to the waters; and you who have no money, come, buy and eat! Come, buy wine and milk without money and without cost.

2 Why spend money on what is not bread, and your labor on what does not satisfy? Listen, listen to me, and eat what is good, and you will delight in the richest of fare. 3 Give ear and

come to me; listen, that you may live. I will make an everlasting covenant with you, my faithful love promised to David. - Isaiah 55:1-3

(NIV)

Reflection Questions

Take a few minutes and think about the following questions. Stop reading, and have a Holy moment with the Father. Allow Him to speak to your heart, Father to son (or daughter). Then, spend a few minutes sharing your heart with the Father.

1. Have I placed my life into Christ's "Fix-it" box? If you have never made a firm decision to follow Christ, there is no better time than now.

2. Have I been worried about something? If so, place that worry in the "Fix-it" box. Christ lovingly teaches us that we do not have to worry.

3. Have I been *trusting* in the Lord or only *believing*? Remember the difference between trust and belief.

Section Two: Art

[My Life in the "Fix-it" Box]

Painting has never been my area of expertise. In fact, art is the only class that I have ever dropped in my entire academic career. Please do not misunderstand. I enjoy, appreciate, and can even say that I love art. I just lack the ability to transform paint and paper into something more than a jumbled rendition of stick figures and multi-colored distortions masquerading as a background.

Despite the fact that I am painting challenged, or maybe because of my lack of artistic ability, I truly appreciate the intricacies and depth of fine works of art. A few years ago, my father and brother traveled to Italy on a business trip. While visiting the Vatican on a free afternoon, they took photographs of some of the most exclusive and masterful works of art on the planet.

When they returned from the trip, I was enthralled with the masterpieces that they had captured on digital film. The sculptures, columns, and opulent tapestries were breathtaking. I was amazed at the precision, depth, and unmatched attention to even the smallest details.

As we were looking through the pictures together, I saw the photograph of the painting on the next page. I was surprised at the hideous appearance and slightly offended that the Vatican, a place that so prides itself on preservation of artifacts, would allow such a masterpiece to deteriorate. Allowing my ignorance to become public, I asked,

"What happened to the picture? Why would they allow it to become damaged?"

My father explained, "There are quite a few works in the Vatican that look like this. The truth is, they are in the process of restoring the paintings."

The painting, a work of art centuries old has withstood pollution, candle wax, and all other sorts of contaminants, leaving it in a darkened and sub-quintessential state not intended by the artist. The restoration work on paintings and masterpieces of art is a science that is tedious, time-consuming, and extraordinarily difficult. Art restorers painstakingly work to remove contaminated material and preserve the masterpiece that the artist originally created.

To my untrained eye, the painting seemed to be in disrepair. This conversation sparked my interest. While preparing to speak at our local youth center, I became fascinated with one of the most important works of art restoration of our time, the restoring of the Sistine Chapel.

The Sistine Chapel

The ceiling of the Sistine Chapel is arguably one of the most beautiful works of art created by mankind. The breathtaking work, painted by the legendary Michelangelo, was completed over a period of four years. For centuries this has been one of the most admired works of human hands. However, over time the beauty and masterwork of Michelangelo began to fade, wear out and was covered by dirt, grime, and wax.

The impressive ceiling was no longer as the artist had originally intended.

After 500 years of use and admiration, in 1980, the Sistine chapel was commissioned to be restored by a team of highly trained art historians and restorers.

This monumental decision was highly controversial in the art world. Many people boldly opposed any attempts at restoring the work. They felt that tampering with the painting in any way could ruin the majesty of Michelangelo's original intentions. To this day, the debate rages throughout the art community, and I am certain that it will continue for many years.

In 1989, the ceiling restoration was finished. (The complete restoration was finished in 1999.) Colors that were once drab, dark, and solemn burst forth in exceptional light. The years of wax, dust, and dirt have been erased from the ceiling revealing a vast array of beauty.

To be sure, the restoration process of the Sistine Chapel was painstakingly tedious. Layers of chemicals and compounds had to be removed from the ceiling without damaging a single priceless brushstroke. The task took years to complete. In the high-paced society in which we live today, very few tedious processes are tolerated. However, this work was priceless. Nothing could be forgotten; not a single step in the restoration process could be skipped or shortened. The work at stake was much too valuable.

It is interesting to me that in the picture shown on page thirty-one, the painting seems to be in a damaged state. It looks as though it is being destroyed and left to its own decay. However, that is not the case! In the end the painting will shine as it was originally intended.

A Broken World...

It does not take much effort to look around the world in which we live and realize that our world is broken and in deep need of true restoration. The grime, dirt, and dingy wax of humanity's selfishness, greed, and self-indulgence is unmistakable in each passing day's headlines. Across the world in every nation on the planet, we encounter need. From single mothers and fathers struggling to provide for their families to wars raging and ravaging the lives of countless people. Suffering is evident in every country, culture, creed, governmental system, and place on earth. Though we live in a time in history where technology and life-saving cures abound and advances in business, commerce and industry are extensive; death and poverty are still present throughout the global society.

We live in a broken world.

It is most certainly true. The world around us is in great need of restoration. Often we can feel this way not only on the macro scale as we look at humanity in general, but also in our own lives. Sometimes our lives are in deep need of the restorative process. I have no idea how many people have said the following statements:

"If I could just go back…"

"If I could only have a second chance…"

"If I could take back those words/actions…"

Sometimes it seems as though life is broken.

When we read the scriptures in Genesis, the Bible is clear that God looked across creation and, "Saw that it was good (Genesis 1:31)." The truth is that although the headlines are often stolen by acts of evil, terror, and selfishness, there are also stories of true human triumph, selfless action, and hope. There are many wonderful people and places in this world. They daily reflect the goodness of God that was originally instilled into humanity.

Michelangelo never intended dirt, candle wax, or smoke to cover and deteriorate his masterpiece. God also did not create humanity with the intention of destruction. Genesis explains that God made man and woman and exclaimed that they were GOOD.

In 2005, when Hurricane Katrina struck, I was a student at Nicholls State University. The storm went on to transform the lives of thousands of people as it wreaked destruction across the Gulf Coast region. Newsrooms were filled with the all too common stories of looting, shootings, and utter chaos. Though these stories did unfortunately occur, I believe that most Louisianans would agree with me that we saw something else during that critical time.

We saw the goodness of humanity on display.

After the storm hit, I watched as community after community banded together to find food, clothing, water, and even shelter for those in need. People gave selflessly, not for their friends or family, but for total and complete strangers. In the midst of the greatest disaster in the history of the United States to date, I saw the divinely designed attributes of God's goodness that are innate in all people who are made in His image.

This was an example of what I believe God intended humanity to look like. We were created for good, not for evil. We were created by God to shine His love to all. This is evident throughout the scriptures. Unfortunately, so often, humanity seems to fall short. Ideals of perfect societies and Utopian philosophies have been the downfall of many. It does seem to be feasible. Is it too late for the restoration of mankind?

Our lives in the "Fix-it" box produce restoration of the soul.

Just as my Father loved to take the time to care and restore each of my toys, so the Father is intent on restoring the genuine "goodness" of humanity. Throughout the Bible, we see the journey of Israel. As they followed the leading of the LORD, often they would turn away from His ways or make egregious errors. However, throughout the scriptures, we see the personality of God revealing Himself as one who desires to restore rather than destroy.

In Revelation 21:5-7, we see the desired outcome of what God has been doing throughout history. His desire is to restore humanity. The beauty of this is that not only is it "humanity" in general, but this includes my life, your life, and anyone who is willing to place their lives in God's hands, namely in His "Fix-it" box.

Revelation 21:5-7

5 And the one sitting on the throne said, "Look, I am making everything new!" And then he said to me, "Write this down, for what I tell you is trustworthy and true." 6 And he also said, "It is finished! I am the Alpha and the Omega—the Beginning and the End. To all who are thirsty I will give freely from the springs of the water of life. 7 All who are victorious will inherit all these blessings, and I will be their God, and they will be my children. – Revelation 21:5-7 (NIV)

When the Sistine Chapel's restoration was completed in 1999, overall, the project was a success. Unfortunately, there was minimal damage to many of the paintings. The eyes of some of the subjects deteriorated, the colors may have been revealed improperly, and many other small details may have been forever lost.

However, when Christ restores, Revelation expresses that there will be no mistakes. Rather than a complete restoration work, the Bible explains that Christ makes us *new*. When Christ works in our lives, He does not just attempt to recover what was lost. Christ re-creates what He desires. The book of Romans (4:17) describes Jehovah as, "The God who calls things that were not as though they were and raises the dead to life." Moreover, Colossians 1:21-22 explains the complete restoring work of Christ in our lives as follows:

21 This includes you who were once far away from God. You were his enemies, separated from him by your evil thoughts and actions. 22 Yet now he has reconciled you to himself through the

death of Christ in his physical body. As a result, he has brought you into his own presence, and you are holy and blameless as you stand before him without a single fault.

Restoration of the Soul

The scriptures clearly express the heart of God not only to restore humanity, but also to personally restore each person. His desire to restore our soul is profoundly expressed on every page of the Bible. In the familiar Psalm, David expresses this wonderful attribute of God,

The Lord is my shepherd; I shall not want.

He makes me to lie down in green pastures;

He leads me beside the still waters.

He restores my soul; - Psalms 23:1-2 (NIV)

It does not matter where we come from, who we are, or what we have done. Christ is clear in His mission. He restores our soul. It is a misconception popularized by mainstream media that Christ is self-centered, small-minded, and angry. The Scripture shows us that His true personality is completely different than what is often thought. His personality and character shout that he loves to restore.

I cannot express my relationship with the Father in clearer terms. Jesus restores my soul. When I mess up; when I fail; when I miss the mark; and when I am guilty; His mercy restores my soul. That is what putting my life in Christ's "Fix-it" box is really all about. He makes my soul whole when it is broken. Through this process, the joy of my life has been found, not in "feeling forgiven," finding purpose, or even realizing that He loves me unconditionally. The joy of my life has been found in KNOWING CHRIST. As I have placed my life in His hands, I have been able to know the King of Kings. What an honor. What a privilege.

Two Obstacles to the Restorative Process

The Bible is clear that God's heart expresses love for all of humanity. Specifically, the Bible forcefully silences rumors that God loves some people more than others. 2 Peter 3:9 incredibly shows the love and patience that Christ has for each person, regardless of who they are, where they are from, or what type background they may have.

9 The Lord is not slow in keeping his promise, as some understand slowness. Instead he is patient with you, not wanting anyone to perish, but everyone to come to repentance. – 2 Peter 3:9 (NIV)

Though the Father desires to restore all men, there are two obstacles that frequently interrupt the restoration process.

1. Stopping the restoration work before it is completed

Flip back a few pages and take a good look at the painting that my brother and father saw in Rome. Can you imagine stopping the restoration work at that stage? It would be utterly disastrous! In fact, in the state shown in the picture, it would have been better never to even begin the restorative process. The work of art would be destroyed.

Quitting the restorative process would be unthinkable.

Sometimes, when I would place my toys in that old

shoebox, I hoped that they would be done in an instant. That was seldom the case! Of course, it takes time to creatively restore toys to their former glory. However, I trusted my father's ability and judgment.

The same process lies true in the restoration of our lives and spirits. When we place our lives in God the Father's spiritual, "Fix-it" box, the restoration process is not instantaneous. To be sure, some aspects of the soul are instantly restored. Joy, peace, and love quickly fill our lives. However, the outward restoration of our actions, attitudes, and sentiments takes the tedious and razor sharp restorative skill of the Holy Spirit.

I have watched many students and friends get discouraged during the restoration process. Be encouraged. The Father is working on our behalf, teaching us to live according to his precepts and principles. However, it is important to realize that it takes time to study the Bible; it takes time to apply these teaching to our lives; and it takes time to learn to hear the Spirit of the Lord prodding and teaching us. In Philippians 3, Paul, imprisoned for his passionate love of Christ, challenges us to keep pushing forward. We must not give up halfway through the restorative process. Do not be discouraged. Take heart and continue to allow the Lord to restore.

12 I don't mean to say that I have already achieved these things or that I have already reached perfection. But I press on to possess that perfection for which Christ Jesus first possessed me. 13 No, dear brothers and sisters, I have not achieved it, but I focus on this one thing: Forgetting the past and looking forward to what lies ahead. Philippians 3:12-13(NLV)

The beauty of Christ's restoration power is that it is not done in *our* power. Christ's work in our lives does not happen because of our own goodness. His work in us is a result of His Spirit, His power, and His grace. Christ first, "Took hold" of us! As Paul further explains in Galatians 6:9, "Let us not become weary while doing well (NIV)." Do not give up! Allow the Lord to continue working in your life.

2. Thinking that God's mercy is limited [AKA: It's too late for me...I tried the "Jesus" thing, but then I messed up again...Will He really restore me again?]

Jesus' restorative power is not limited to our understanding of mercy and grace. The Bible says, "His mercy is new every morning (Lamentations 3:23)!" I am ever grateful for His love and mercy in my life. I am so glad that even when I make mistakes, Christ's restorative power still works on my behalf. He never excludes us from the "Fix-it" box.

There is a story in the Bible that illustrates this mercy and grace brilliantly. In 1 Kings 16, we meet one of the most heinous and evil characters in the Bible. His name is King Ahab. The introductory scriptures about this man solidify his villainous stature.

1 Kings 16:29-33 (NIV):

29 In the thirty-eighth year of Asa king of Judah, Ahab son of Omri became king of Israel, and he reigned in Samaria over Israel twenty-two years. 30 Ahab son of Omri did more evil in the eyes of the Lord than any of those before him. 31 He not only considered it trivial to commit the sins of Jeroboam son of Nebat, but he also married Jezebel daughter of Ethbaal king of the

Sidonians, and began to serve Baal and worship him. 32 He set up an altar for Baal in the temple of Baal that he built in Samaria. 33 Ahab also made an Asherah pole and <u>did more to arouse the anger of the Lord, the God of Israel, than did all the kings of Israel before him.</u>

Wow! How is that for an introduction? I do not think the name "Ahab" ever made it onto the "most popular baby names" list. This man was EVIL. He literally changed the spiritual course of an entire nation. It would seem obvious that Ahab was beyond God's restorative touch. However, searching the scriptures gives us a surprising look into the character of our Father. It clearly shows God's heart to restore even the most unlikely of people.

In 2 Kings 20, we see the incredible story of a battle between King Ahab and an alliance of thirty-two kings. The odds were completely against evil king Ahab. However, in a moment of stunning grace and mercy, God moved on Ahab's behalf and gave him a miraculous and impossible victory. Not only once, but twice, the evil king is given divine victory over his enemies. Why? How could this be? Why would God allow an evil man to succeed in battle in a time when victory was synonymous with God's favor? The answer is simple.

1 Kings 20:13 (NIV)

13 Meanwhile a prophet came to Ahab king of Israel and announced, "This is what the Lord says: 'Do you see this vast army? I will give it into your hand today, and <u>then you will know that I am the Lord.</u>'"

Even though King Ahab was one of the most evil kings that ever lived, God the Father wanted to give him a chance to see His power, ability, and love.

Even Ahab, the worst man in Israel's history, was important to God the Father.

Sadly, after the great victory, Ahab still refused to serve the Lord. He soon died in his evil ways. However, that does not change the fact that God showed his power to Ahab. I believe that He was offering to restore him and teach him to live in righteousness. Though Ahab failed, this story has massive implications for us today. It proclaims to all generations that the Father's heart is to restore anyone who is willing. We are never too far-gone for His mercy. The obstacle to restoration lies with us. God the Father is willing. The question is, "Are we willing to allow him to restore our lives?"

Reflection Questions

Take a few minutes and think about the following questions. Stop reading, and have a Holy moment with the Father. Allow Him to speak to your heart, Father to son (or daughter). Then, spend a few minutes sharing your heart with the Father.

1. Are there areas in my life that need the restoration power of Christ? If so, which areas?

2. Have I been discouraged because the restoration process sometimes takes longer than I expected?

3. Have you ever felt like you were "too far-gone" to be restored? If so, take a minute and thank God for His constant mercy and undying love for you.

Section Three: Cross-Country

[My Exhaustion in the "Fix-it" Box]

The starting pistol sounded, and my mind quickly raced back to the events preceding the beginning of the 2001 district cross-country 5k. How in the world did I arrive here? It was the first time that I had ever been selected to compete at an "actual" cross-country running event for my high school team. Why the coach decided to test my skills and athleticism at the district-level championship was beyond my understanding, but I was determined to do my best.

This being my first race, I was a bit on edge. As my teammates chugged bottles of honey or talked about their pre-race routines, I wandered around the stadium at Assumption High School. I had no idea what to do next. However, the time finally came to head to the starting line.

Nervously, I gathered with my friends and waited for the start. As the race began, I shot out with all of my might, thinking, "No Jacob...pace yourself! All you have to do is not finish dead last." Surprisingly, things seemed to be going well. I quickly settled into a rhythm at what I assumed to be the middle of the proverbial pack. In a group of about twenty boys, I ran with all of my heart. As we finished out what I think was the first half kilometer, my cross-country coach yelled out a quick, "Good job, Noel! Keep on going!" To which I responded, "Thanks, Coach!" As I passed, my coach's voice faded behind me, "Ha, don't respond! Just run!" I am sure I heard the crowd snickering at the newbie in the group.

"I guess this isn't the place for pleasantries," I thought, as I put my head down and continued plodding forward.

As we continued through the five-kilometer course, I noticed that there were fewer and fewer runners around me. Where once nearly twenty mediocre runners fought to cross the finish line, now only ten were at my side. With each passing moment, another student would throw in the towel and walk towards the locker room. Focusing on my own race, I continued to run. Soon, I looked up again and noticed only a few stragglers with me. Somewhat disappointed, but not discouraged, I continued on towards the goal.

As time passed, many of the runners in my group began to grumble. I heard plenty of common complaints.

"I'm giving up."

"This is ridiculous."

"I didn't really feel like trying today; otherwise I would be in first place."

With each complaint another runner slowed to a walk and headed home. Finally, I ran with a group of only three other boys. The somewhat humiliating sounds of others crossing the finish line to a roaring crowd filled our ears albeit from quite a distance. However, none of that really mattered to me. This was my very first race, and I came to finish.

At this point in the event, race organizers began collecting mile-markers and by the time we reached the water station before the last kilometer, only a sea of strewn paper cups lined the grass (or at least that is the way it felt). We were the last four runners in the race.

As we approached the final field, I could hear the beating of my own heart reverberating in my eardrums, and my breathing was so hard, I think everyone waiting at the finish line nearly half a kilometer away must have heard it. As we began to run around the field, a friend of mine spoke up, "Guys," he gasped, "I'm not running anymore. No one is here, the line judges are all gone, and no one cares what we do. I am not running around the field. I am going to cut through it and finish the race now. No one will see or care if we finish the complete five kilometers."

The other boys running with me concurred that this plan seemed to be the best option, and besides, no one would be humiliated by finishing last if we all finished together. However, I couldn't do it. "No way," I gasped as I fought to keep my legs moving. "We have run this far; I want to finish the race."

With a smirk, the boys ran the other way.

The embarrassing implications of this decision had yet to occur to me. I clung to the slight hope that I would pass some other kid as I picked up my pace for the final leg of the race. However, my fears were fully realized as I ran into the empty stadium at Assumption High School.

In the feared "dead last" position, I ran with all of my might to finish my first five-kilometer race. My mother was there to meet me with a smile and exclaimed, "You did it! You finished!"

Even though I finished last to the eerie quiet of a nearly empty stadium, I was filled with joy. I had never run so far before, and I knew that some had quit, others had cheated, and I knew that this race was well beyond my skill level. I was proud to finish.

As my mother and I talked about my experience, one of the boys who had crossed the finish line shortly before I did came over to me. With an uncomfortable look he congratulated me on a "race well run." His face told it all. The idea to cheat and cut across the open field had once seemed so obvious, but in this moment he couldn't hide his disappointment in his choice.

Have you ever been tired?

As I look back on my brief running career, I realize that the entire race was pretty comical, but I cannot help but see how the race parallels with everyday life. It does not matter who you are; every one of us gets tired. We run with great vigor and excitement in our life at times, and then at other times, it seems like every step is exhausting. If you are tired as you read this page, I just want to encourage you.

Don't give up.

We have all been there. We have all been tired, ready to quit, and just fed up with what seems like effort that is wasted, unnoticed, and ineffective.

Don't give up.

Maybe you started out hoping for change, with bright ideas and new concepts that surely would make an impact on the world around you. However, coworkers, friends, and even family soon began to discourage your journey.

Don't give up.

As a Christian, I am convinced that often times, people are set upon the journey that the Lord has placed before them, a journey of destiny and divine purpose, but they grow tired along the way. The difficulties of the daily grind or journey begin to burn like the lactic acid buildup in the muscles of an untrained distance runner. The all too familiar excuses of those around us begin to resound in our ears.

"I'm giving up."

"This is ridiculous."

"Is this really even worth all of the effort that I am investing?"

As we push forward in our lives, and grow more

and more tired by the moment, the final lie comes head-on.

"No one will notice if you just give up. No one is even paying attention to your life or journey or dream."

The temptation to cheat ourselves out of the true and matchless plan that the Lord has for us begins to seem so logical.

Don't give up.

There is Hope, namely Christ, and He has promised that He will be with us until the end. The Scriptures are clear in the fact that "He who began a good work in me is faithful to complete it! (Philippians 1:6). Often when we are ready to quit, the finish line is only half a kilometer away. More importantly, the Lord's promise is not a dead last finish. It is a Crown of Life and overwhelming victory.

7 I have fought the good fight, I have finished the race, I have kept the faith. 8 Now there is in store for me the crown of righteousness, which the Lord, the righteous Judge, will award to me on that day—and not only to me, but also to all who have longed for his appearing.

-2 Timothy 4:7-8 (NIV)

What do we do when we are ready to quit?

I am convinced that in today's world, many come to Christ under an erroneous pretense that states that everything will be better if you have Christ in your life. Surely, a life filled with Christ is a better life, but there are no promises that the situations we face will get easier, less difficult, and smoother. In fact the scripture is filled with just the opposite promise.

Why then, would we desire Christ? It is because He fills us with His strength, His ability, His compassion for the lost, and His wisdom to overcome difficulties.

However, in the middle of the exhaustion, what are we to do?

We must put our exhaustion in the "Fix-it" box of Christ.

I would suggest that we study one of the most important scriptures for living out a Christ-like life in the midst of exhaustion: Hebrews 12:1-2. In this verse we can see three clear ways that we can place our exhaustion in the Father's "Fix-it" box.

Therefore we also, since we are surrounded by so great a cloud of witnesses, let us lay aside every weight, and the sin which so easily ensnares *us*, and let us run with endurance the race that is set before us, 2 looking unto Jesus, the author and finisher of *our* faith, who for the joy that was set before Him endured the cross, despising the shame, and has sat down at the right hand of the throne of God.

- Hebrews 12:1-2 (NIV)

1. Strip off every weight and sin...

There are weights in our lives and sins that do easily slow us down aren't there? The full and abundant life that Jesus promises in the Scriptures is not possible if we are weighted down. Imagine an Olympic athlete running the 400-meter dash carrying a 100lb backpack. Surely the lightning fast results of years of training would be slowed to that of almost the common man. We were designed to live free of the sin and weights that often willingly carry on a daily basis.

Sin...

In 1 John 1:9, there is a verse of particular freedom. The Bible explains that when we confess our sins, Christ is faithful to forgive us [completely]. (Paraphrase). Christ's forgiveness is complete, whole, and total. The work that He did on the cross was finished and does not need to be repeated. His forgiveness is enough to cover our wrongdoings.

When we hold on to sin in our lives, it has a tendency to slow down our progress not only spiritually but in every area. When our spirit is troubled, everything that we do, from schoolwork to grocery shopping to working in the corporate office, will suffer. Exhaustion and lackadaisical living multiply in the presence of sin.

As you read this, if you have been struggling with sin, I want you to take a minute, put this book down, and take a Holy Moment with the Lord. Confess your sin to the Lord and ask Him to clean you of all unrighteousness. I do not know what sin may be your struggle, but I want you to know that the Lord is enough to free you from that sin's power over your life. Sins of pride (thinking of yourself as better than others), arrogance (shouting of your own greatness rather than the Father's love), selfishness (placing our own desires over the needs of others), gossip (sharing our opinion about others difficulties or struggles with other people), slander (purposely defaming others), or any other sin that may be in your heart or mind are instantly forgiven as we confess them to the Lord and trust in His saving mercy.

Isn't His presence amazing? I love the peace that Christ can bring into the midst of chaos. When our hearts are filled with guilt and shame, Christ's forgiveness brings everlasting Hope.

Forgiveness is a real and active process. The Bible explains that we no longer need to rehash our old mistakes and sins, but rather, when they are given to Christ, the battle is finished. We are truly and completely clean. In fact, in Romans 8, the scripture explains that any "condemnation" or rehashing of our mistakes is definitively not from the Lord!

Weights...

There are many things that can weigh us down in life. Of course, sin easily ensnares, but I think there is a difference between the sin and weights listed in the Hebrews 12. Weights are things that people have spoken about us, our own inability to forgive ourselves for failures or shortcomings, or anything else that takes our peace.

The enemy of our soul would love to have us carrying unnecessary weights in the race that Christ has set before us. The scriptures even call him the "Accuser of the brethren." However, I want to remind you that these accusations are not true accusations; they are false. We are the masterpiece of Christ created to do good work (see Chapter 4).

Maybe you have been carrying unnecessary weights in your life. If you have been heavy-laden with painful words that others have spoken over your life, please know that the words of others do not define who we are. We are the righteousness of God in Christ Jesus (2 Corinthians 5:21), and though we have yet to reach perfection, we are free to throw off the weights of the lies and hurts that other people want us to carry.

Just take a quick moment and if you have been carrying unnecessary weights, I want to invite you to hand those things over to Jesus Christ. The Bible even says in 1 Peter 5:7, "Cast your cares upon Him, for He cares for you." Notice that Christ doesn't take our cares or burdens because He is strong. He doesn't take our burdens because He is able. He doesn't take our burdens because He is Creator. He takes our burdens because He *cares* for us. Cast your weights upon Him, and run the race that Christ has set before you.

Don't give up.

2. Surround yourself with a 'cloud of witnesses'

In the eleventh chapter of Hebrews, an entire list of heroes of Christian faith is listed. This list is commonly known as the "Hall of Faith." (Which reminds me of the Justice League for some reason...smile.) In this incredible listing of Biblical heroes, the author of Hebrews is expressing the truth that it is important to remember those who have gone before us and walked in the victory of Christ. "Since we are surrounded by so great a cloud of witnesses," is a statement that expresses the idea that we are not alone in Christ! We must remember what God has done! In the difficult situations of others, God has been faithful! Through difficult trials, tribulations, and even in death, Christ is with us.

When I am exhausted and ready to give up, there is an important principle to apply to our lives from the "cloud of witnesses" reference. When we are going through struggles, we must be careful who we allow to surround us. Think about this for minute. We all have groups of friends or people that exude optimism, grace, mercy, and joy. When I surround myself with such people, the outlook of my own situation begins to change shape, and I am filled with passion to attack every difficulty and find victory in Christ.

However, the antithesis of this situation is extraordinarily common. Let me illustrate this with a fictional example from life in the hospital...

Fictional County Hospital...

In the midst of a bustling emergency department, the nursing staff runs in and out of patient's rooms starting IV's, administering medications, or even working on the code team. Things can get hectic to say the least.

Tanya, a young nurse who is tired from a long shift glances at her watch and sighs. Sheila, while catching up on charting simply asks, "Tanya, pass me the stapler?"

However, as the night-shift-induced fatigue sets in on young Tanya, she actually hears, "TANYA, PASS ME THE STAPLER!"

(Please note the difference in punctuation. Sheila asked, "Pass me the Stapler?" but Tanya hears, "Pass me the stapler!")

"Pass her the Stapler?" Tanya thought, "Who does she think she is telling me to pass her a stapler! How demanding!"

Then, a perturbed and tired Tanya heads to the break room to take her fifteen-minute lunch break. While inside, she encounters John, the unit's respiratory therapist. Quickly, she spreads her "cheer" to John, who in turn begins to harbor ill feelings towards that demanding, overbearing stapler-hogging Sheila. John then proceeds to the post-op surgery unit and shares his newfound frustration with Dr. Wilder, the chief of surgery. Before long all of Fictional County Hospital is furious at Sheila, who in all honesty only asked to borrow a stapler.

I am fascinated and acutely aware of the fact that aggravation, frustration, and tiredness seem to travel quickly in groups of people. If we surround ourselves with such people when we are tired, we are even more at risk to lose sight of the Crown Victory that Christ has promised to those who run the race with endurance. As in my cross-country experience, it was much easier for the other runners to quit when they did not quit alone.

Thankfully, I believe that joy, laughter, and faith also spread easily. When we are tired and worn out, it is imperative to have good fellowship that will encourage and strengthen our heart in order to continue toward the prize that Christ has set before us as believers. We must surround ourselves with a "Great cloud of witnesses."

3. When we are tired, we must focus our eyes on Christ, the Author and Finisher of our faith.

When we are tired, we often lose perspective. Quickly, what once seemed like a faith-filled adventure to accomplish the impossible seems as though it is a forsaken quest to achieve something elusive. When running a race, the lactic acid buildup in muscles causes neurons to fire with such intensity that rest seems the only logical course of action. Thoughts of winning a race or even finishing a long-distance race begin to seem downright silly. Quickly, in the midst of tired muscles, burning lungs, and a sweat-drenched brow, giving up seems to be the best option. Our natural tendency is to forget the great prize at the finish line.

However, as Christians, living out the wondrous calling of Christ to share His love with all we meet, we cannot forget about the prize that we have been promised. The prize for which we run is not a wreath of olive branches, a trophy, or even a title. We run to win a Crown of righteousness!

Crown of Righteousness

The great prize of our race is righteousness. The Bible explains in 2 Corinthians 5:21,

For He made Him who knew no sin *to be* sin for us, that we might become the righteousness of God in Him – 2 Corinthians 5:21 (NKJV)

Christ is the great reward. He is our great prize. My prize is not going to church. My prize is not religion. My prize is not money, fame, fortune, provision, or healing. Christ is my great reward. He is my great prize. In Him I am whole. In Him I am strong. In Christ I am the righteousness of God in Christ Jesus!

When tiredness and discouragement overcome our hearts, we must set our eyes upon the prize. The prize of knowing Christ is unmatched throughout the universe. He is the highest prize. There is no other way to describe the incredible love of Christ except that He is the One who makes my soul whole. Where others leave us broken, or where joy and happiness seem temporary, Christ makes my soul whole. He is the one who covers my mistakes, redeems my past, and gives me purpose for today, tomorrow, and forever.

The Author and Finisher of our Faith...

I really love this phrase in the Scriptures. When we realize that Christ is the Author and the Finisher of our very faith, everything in our understanding of religion quickly changes. Our Faith is not ours to design, to invent, to interpret, or to discover. Christ is the One who authored our faith. He is the One who will reveal Himself to us through His precious Holy Spirit.

Interestingly, He is not only the creator of our understanding of Himself, but Christ is the Finisher of our Faith! Did you catch that? If Christ is the Finisher of our Faith, then that frees me from the unnecessary burden of working continuously to perfect my own faith. In Christ, I am free to allow Him to work in me! I am not bound to daily struggle of hoping that I can figure out my own faith! I can trust in the Lord and allow Him to develop faith in me, knowing and trusting confidently that He is the one who is more than able to finish. When my eyes are set upon Christ, I need not be distracted or slowed with relying on my own knowledge or ability to understand faith. I can freely trust that He is enough to strengthen me to persevere to the end. We need not give up. We can focus our eyes on Christ the Author and the Finisher of our Faith!

Reflection Questions

Take a few minutes and think about the following questions. Stop reading, and have a Holy moment with the Father. Allow Him to speak to your heart, Father to son (or daughter). Then, spend a few minutes sharing your heart with the Father.

1. Have I been exhausted lately? Why?

2. Have I felt like giving up on something that the Father has put on my heart to do? If so, why?

3. Which point(s) in this chapter do I need to apply to my life?

Chapter 4

From Blocks to Buildings

[My Dreams in the "Fix-it" Box]

As a child, I can remember gazing upon the beauty of numerous boxes that gleamed with tales of adventure and intrigue throughout the toy aisle. From G.I. Joe's escapades against Cobra Commander to the creative mischief of a Creepy Crawler's workshop, adventure was mine to be had.

Occasionally, my brother and I had the oft longed-for opportunity to choose a new toy. We both loved to play with Legos. With astronauts that explored the far reaches of the galaxy, pirates to pillage and plunder the seas, and aquanauts to discover the depths of the oceans, Legos provide riveting entertainment for young minds the world over.

However, I now must admit that I have a confession to make. I greatly enjoyed playing with Legos, but a secret that has been with me for many years, is that I never really enjoyed *building* them. I realize that the engineers behind such toys marketed them with the intent that I would enjoy the building process, but I much preferred playing with the finished product. Thus, while my brother labored at the tedious and arduous process of completing the structures, I either stared at the box imagining the delights of coming capers or played with the toys "we" had previously built.

I really enjoyed the imaginative play of the constructed toy. I was excited about the prospects of new adventures with spaceships, castles or pirate boats. However, sometimes going from blocks to buildings proved to be tedious, trying, and difficult.

The process of building a Lego set actually begins long before a child opens the box and pours the blocks all over the floor (much to the dismay of parents who enjoy walking around in only socks). The makers of Lego toys are acutely aware that the journey to building the newest Lego castle actually begins with the picture on the toy's box. The box designs for the Lego company are literally works of art. Each set seems to come to life on the cardboard as misty clouds hang over the tops of ancient Lego castles, and intense battle sequences seem to be unfolding on the front of the package.

Upon arriving home and opening the box, seemingly countless pieces and intricate blocks fall towards the floor. To me, this represents the tedious process that awaits until the real fun can be had in the final product. Finally, after many hours (or minutes if you are not Lego-challenged), the finished product is ready to be enjoyed! This process is quite extensive!

In our lives, we often have a picture of something that we would like to accomplish, but it is very difficult to leave our known life and strive to accomplish something new. We may have an idea or a dream, but as we begin walking toward what we wish to accomplish, it seems as though there are so many pieces that must be put together. In essence, our dream seems to be a pile of Lego blocks. How do we move from blocks to buildings?

Identity Check...

Just as Legos are designed with a purpose, each set

is designed to form a specific vehicle or type of adventure. In the same way, we too are made in the image of God and have a determined purpose. Scripture affirms people are formed in the womb with specific purposes in mind (Psalm 139), and that God's plans for us are known (Jeremiah 1:5).

That being said, rather than fulfilling the purposes and dreams that God has established for our lives, people frequently believe the following lies or expressions of self-pity:

"Other people can do great things, but I just don't have the talent or ability."

It must be amazing to be able to serve God, but I don't know how."

"Too bad I can't serve in my local church. I'm just not holy, like those other people."

"Too bad I can't make a difference in my community."

Ephesians 2:10 speaks directly to these deceptions.

"For we are God's masterpiece. He has created us anew in Christ so we can do the good things he planned for us long ago (NLT)."

This is an absolutely astounding statement. We are the masterpiece of Christ! *We* are God's greatest work. Not only are we prized and loved, but we are also given a clear purpose: to do good work. This good work, evident as we follow Christ, is also expressed in 1 Peter 2:9.

"...For you are a chosen people. You are royal priests, a holy nation, God's very own possession. As a result, you can show others the

goodness of God, for he called you out of the darkness into his wonderful light."

It is evident that we are called to do good work. God has planned the good things that we are to do long in advance! This is not self-help egotistical thinking. This is the reality of life expressed in the Scriptures! Moreover, not only are we called to do good work, but also we are called to do *Kingdom* work. The things that we are called to do in life are of eternal significance and purpose! Part of our identity in Christ is knowing that we are a "holy nation" that represents Christ to those around us. Everything we do, say, and create represents Jesus Christ to others.

Good work is different than Kingdom work. Kingdom work is actually good works that are done in the Name of Jesus Christ. All of humanity has the capacity to do good work. Helping those in need is good work. However, Kingdom work is work done to specifically share the Love of Christ with mankind.

If our purpose is clear, as expressed previously, then why do so many fail to live out the dream that is placed upon their hearts? It is possible to live without ever fulfilling the purpose that God has intended. Sometimes, we see an idea of what we would like to do (a picture on the Lego box). It seems amazing. Maybe it is a calling to a certain career type that would allow more opportunities to share the Gospel, or maybe a calling to serve more in the local church, or even a call to the mission field or full-time service for Christ. I believe every person has felt the desire to live a life that is effective for Christ.

This dream is like a box of Legos. We see a beautiful picture of what our life could look like.

We see something amazing on the cover of the box. However, often when we begin to explore the dream, we open a box and see so many intricate pieces. This box of a dream with all of its tiny blocks seems as though it will take forever to build into Christ's vision for our lives.

There are many examples in the Bible of men and women who accomplished the dreams that God had placed in their heart. They effectively built a building from the blocks that God had given them. David's story of a life that transitioned from the life of a shepherd to a warrior to king is an excellent example of what it means to build from blocks to buildings.

Spoiler alert! David kills Goliath.

I think every young boy who has ever heard the

story of David and Goliath, has pictured himself on a dusty battlefield armed with a sling against an astounding foe. This story of seemingly impossible victory resonates with everyone, regardless of culture, creed, or country. Humankind loves the idea of victory for the underdog.

Before we begin the story, we should understand one important implication of the epic battle between the giant Goliath and the young boy, David. This style of fighting, "Battle by champion," placed one champion from each army against the other. It was believed that the champions fought not through their own might, but that the god of each army would determine the outcome of the battle. Therefore, when David stepped out to fight against Goliath, it was not a statement of his own strength. Rather, it was statement of faith. David trusted in Jehovah to win the impossible victory and bring honor to His name.

Let's look at the events leading up to the historic battle...

David, a young boy of probably sixteen or seventeen, generally spent his time working as a shepherd. While his brothers were away at the now infamous battle, his father requested that he bring food to them and retrieve news of their well-being. I can imagine that any teenager would jump at the chance to leave their chores with others and visit older siblings at the battle lines. David was no exception. Let's pick up the story there.

1 Samuel 17:20-26

20 Early in the morning David left the flock in the care of a shepherd, loaded up and set out, as Jesse had directed. He reached the camp as the army was going out to its battle positions,

shouting the war cry. 21 Israel and the Philistines were drawing up their lines facing each other. 22 David left his things with the keeper of supplies, ran to the battle lines and asked his brothers how they were. 23 As he was talking with them, Goliath, the Philistine champion from Gath, stepped out from his lines and shouted his usual defiance, <u>and David heard it</u>. 24 Whenever the Israelites saw the man, they all fled from him in great fear.

25 Now the Israelites had been saying, "Do you see how this man keeps coming out? He comes out to defy Israel. The king will give great wealth to the man who kills him. He will also give him his daughter in marriage and will exempt his family from taxes in Israel."

26 David asked the men standing near him, "What will be done for the man who kills this Philistine and removes this disgrace from Israel? <u>Who is this uncircumcised Philistine that he should defy the armies of the living God?</u>"

1. Holy Discontentment

Here, David begins to see the picture of what God wants to do. He, in essence, sees the picture on the Lego box. He sees something of great importance that can and should be done. He is frustrated by the lack of action of others and by the unjust action of the enemy. Often times in our lives, we wait for God to speak a clear and audible direction for us. However, many times God's direction for our lives does not come from supernatural experiences (though sometimes it does). Often, God's purposes for our lives rise out of what a friend of mine refers to as "Holy Discontentment."

Tim Bebee, a dear friend with whom Amanda and I were privileged to work alongside of in El Salvador, once explained to me how the Lord called him into mission work. For many years both he and his wife worked as respiratory therapists and loved their jobs. They were highly successful in what they were doing, and the work was important. They constantly worked to save lives and to care for the sick. However, the Lord began to speak to Tim through an increasing desire to leave his job behind and serve the Lord in a new capacity overseas. This "Holy Discontentment" began to stir in him and in his wife daily. What was once joyful and exhilarating began to be replaced by the desire to step out in faith and serve the Lord. It began as a small "Holy Discontentment." What had once been extremely rewarding began to seem mundane. Tim began to long to serve the Lord in a greater way. Over time, this "Holy Discontentment" gradually grew into the picture of what the Lord had planned for this incredible family. Soon after, they left everything they knew in the United States to serve Lord in El Salvador. After four and a half years of giving their all in Central America, the Lord has yet again moved them, and they now serve the Lord worldwide through a ministry named Compassions

Call.

I believe this same "Holy Discontentment" is present when people, who were once content with only belonging to church, begin to feel the Holy Spirit's leading to do more and become involved; to begin sharing their faith with others; or maybe even to begin using their divinely given talents and abilities to impact their cities, states, countries, and the world for the Kingdom of God. When "Holy Discontentment" envelops our heart, church no longer consists of only a social obligation. Rather, it becomes a life-giving Body of Christ that joyously reaches out to impact anyone and everyone.

In order to begin to build blocks into buildings, in essence, to move towards the dream that the Lord has put into our heart, we must recognize "Holy Discontentment." It is important to note that there is a difference between "Holy Discontentment" that leads toward action and complaining which leads to nothing. There is a marked difference between the two. "Holy Discontentment" will lead you to life whereas complaining seems to suck the life out of everyone!

2. Opposition

As David is filled with "Holy Discontentment" about the situation of the Philistine, he begins to rise to action. However, it is not long before opposition to his courage and faith arrives with fierce vigor.

28When Eliab, David's oldest brother, heard him speaking with the men, he burned with anger at him and asked, "Why have you come down here? <u>And with whom did you leave those few sheep in the wilderness?</u> I know how conceited you are and how wicked your heart is;

you came down only to watch the battle."

29 "Now what have I done?" said David. "Can't I even speak?" - 1 Samuel 17:28-29 (NIV)

Why is it that Eliab was so angry with David? I think it is because Eliab may have seen the very same "picture" or had the very same dream that David had. Eliab may very well have felt in his heart the same "Holy Discontentment" with the current situation. However, Eliab lacked the faith necessary to put his desires into action. Therefore, when David was moved to action, Eliab felt the sting of realizing that he should have been the one to respond to the taunts of the Philistine. Could it be that Eliab felt the same call from God to stop the Philistine? I think so. However rather than admitting his own unwillingness to act, he lashed out at his brother.

Notice that the attack against David was not only

discouraging, it was intensely personal. David was a shepherd. The sheep that he kept were his long-term responsibility. David spent hours with the sheep. Eliab knew that this verbal jab would hurt.

In our lives, when we take a step toward action to fulfill the purposes that God has called us to, we will find opposition.

In 1 Samuel 17:31-33, the story continues.

31 Then David's question was reported to King Saul, and the king sent for him.

32 "Don't worry about this Philistine," David told Saul. "I'll go fight him!"

33 "Don't be ridiculous!" Saul replied. "There's no way you can fight this Philistine and possibly win! You're only a boy, and he's been a man of war since his youth."

Ouch! "Don't be ridiculous?" What a difficult opposition to overcome! The king of the entire land opposes David's God-given dream. The implication is staggering. Saul's response carries the power to completely and totally deny David the ability to accomplish what he has henceforth felt was a Holy Spirit-led action.

Whenever the Call of the Lord comes upon our life to do something for the Kingdom of God, people will often stand up and say, "Don't be ridiculous!" However, please understand that facing opposition does not mean that God has not placed the dream for action in your heart. Opposition is a normal part of moving from blocks to buildings. Opposition can be used as a weapon from the enemy to block the dream of God from effectively being constructed. Do not be discouraged when opposition comes.

David does not allow Saul to shake his conviction.

But David persisted. "I have been taking care of my father's sheep and goats," he said. "When a lion or a bear comes to steal a lamb from the flock, 35 I go after it with a club and rescue the lamb from its mouth. If the animal turns on me, I catch it by the jaw and club it to death. 36 I have done this to both lions and bears, and I'll do it to this pagan Philistine, too, for he has defied the armies of the living God! 37 The Lord who rescued me from the claws of the lion and the bear will rescue me from this Philistine!"

Saul finally consented. "All right, go ahead," he said. "And may the Lord be with you!"

Awesome.

It is interesting to note that there is no arrogance in

David's description of his previous exploits. He is clear about one thing. It was the LORD who rescued him from the lion and the bear. The LORD fought his battles in the past, and David was confident that the LORD would do it again.

To David, this was not just a battle. Fighting Goliath was a step of faith. When Saul noted David's faith, he finally allowed him to prepare for battle. This faith was not manufactured on the spot. David's unquenchable faith in the LORD came from his time in the fields as a shepherd.

3. Do Not Despise Unique Preparation

In Biblical times, working as a shepherd was not a high-class job. It was dirty, tiring work. David spent long hours outdoors, and the social standing of shepherds in Biblical times was questionable at best. In fact, in 1 Samuel 16, when the prophet Samuel came to David's father's house to anoint the new king of Israel, no one even thought to tell David, who was out in the fields with the sheep.

While David's brothers were out to war, representing their country and serving the king, David was left behind in the fields. However, David did not despise his time of preparation. Rather, he embraced the time he had in the fields. David became a skilled warrior protecting his sheep from the predators of the area. If we read through the Psalms, it is quite obvious that David's time in the fields instilled in him a heart like that of the Father.

Moreover, David's time of preparation as a shepherd prepared him to face the fight of his life. 1 Samuel 17:38-40

38 Then Saul gave David his own armor—a bronze helmet and a coat of mail. 39 David put it on, strapped the sword over it, and took a step or two to see what it was like, for he had never worn such things before.

"I can't go in these," he protested to Saul. "I'm not used to them." So David took them off again. 40 He picked up five smooth stones from a stream and put them into his shepherd's bag. Then, armed only with his shepherd's staff and sling, he started across the valley to fight the Philistine.

When I came across this scripture, I realized that God's plans for us involve individually unique preparation. We must go in the strength of the Lord, utilizing the unique preparation that God has given to each of us. Often people are in anguish about their calling because they think as follows:

"I want to serve the Lord. If I was just like that person (insert name of your hero here), then I would be successful!"

"I wish I could be more like my pastor or leader. Then I could really accomplish God's calling on my life, but as myself, I won't be victorious!"

Some people feel called to do something specific, whether in life or in ministry and spend their efforts trying to fit into the mold that has been set by others as they fulfilled God's call on their lives. However, God prepares each person uniquely! David could not go to battle in Saul's armor, and I am certain that Saul could not fight a battle with a sling and a stone!

Similarly, I cannot preach my pastor's message. I cannot live out my brother's calling. I cannot fulfill the destiny of someone else. I have to be who God called *me* to be; and I have to do so the *way* that He calls me so that I can uniquely complete the good, Kingdom work He has created me to do.

David took his sling and his staff and stood before a nine-foot-tall giant. When he took that impossible step using the preparation that God had given him, the Bible explains that God received the glory. It was totally unexpected that a teenager with a sling could kill a battle-hardened giant. However, when David moved in the strength of the Lord, He defeated the giant and achieved the impossible. In that moment David's God-given dream turned from blocks into a building. It became a reality.

Do not be discouraged if you do not think you have the capacity to accomplish what the Lord has set before you. My talents are different than yours. Your giftings are different than mine, but when the

Lord calls us to act, He will ensure that the needed preparation, as unique as it may be, is in place.

Is it too late?

If God has called us to something, it is possible and even probable that along the way we will make mistakes. God does not crush dreams. We can place our dreams in the fix-it box of Christ at any point. It does not matter if you are young or old. If the dreams that God has placed in our heart to build are only halfway built, it is never too late to pick up the blocks again and start working for the Kingdom anew.

Many people have had the moment of holy discontentment, made it through opposition, and maybe began to build the dream that the Lord has given them, but then along the way got tired, quit, or made a mistake. Their dream may seem destroyed or broken because of a mistake, but I want to encourage you. Put your dreams in Christ's "Fix-it" box. Allow the Father to mend His dreams for you and put them back together. Ideas and pictures and dreams of beautiful families and relationships may have broken apart, but Christ, in His Fatherly love can rejuvenate any dream. It doesn't matter if it is too far-gone.

There is still hope.

If you have failed in a dream that the Lord has given you,

There is still hope!

If you feel like it is too late to serve the Lord and you are too old to fix your mistakes, do not lose heart.

There is still hope!

Our God is a Father who does not only restore dreams. He restores families, relationships, and especially our souls. Even now, if you are in need of His touch, put this book down and spend time in His presence. If you have been wandering through life hoping for a purpose, ask the Lord to begin to give you "Holy Discontentment"; to allow you to persevere through opposition; and to utilize your unique and special preparation in order to fulfill the dream He has created you to do. He has created us to turn blocks into glorious and beautiful buildings.

Reflection Questions

Take a few minutes and think about the following questions. Stop reading, and have a Holy moment with the Father. Allow Him to speak to your heart, Father to son (or daughter). Then, spend a few minutes sharing your heart with the Father.

1. Am I doing all that God has called me to do for Him?

2. Have I felt "Holy Discontentment" in my life lately? If so, why?

3. Are there dreams that I need to place in the "Fix-it" box? (Are there things that God called me to do long ago that I have forgotten, neglected, or ignored?)

Section 5

Rickshaws, Palaces, and Chai

[Love in the "Fix-it" Box]

India is a fascinating land. From rich colors that shine brightly across desert cities to the highest spires of ornately decorated palaces, India is absolutely thrilling to behold. Amanda and I have had the opportunity to travel to many places across the world. When my parents asked, "How is India?" I was literally without words. Describing this land so steeped in rich culture and wondrous beauty would take hours. Moreover, I completely lack the words to express what it feels like to walk the streets of the sub-continent. However, I will try to give you a glimpse into India.

Truth be told, I don't think India can truly be experienced without certain events. If you ever find yourself in the beautiful land of India, it is imperative to note the following:

1. Driving at breakneck speeds through crowded streets on a Hero-Honda motorcycle with a minimum of two other passengers (a total of three...for a more conventional experience, one passenger must sit "side-saddle") is the best way to truly experience travel in India.

2. Tasting the wonders of Indian cuisine is a must! Foods must include the likes of panipuri (a small fried shell that is dipped into various "flavored" waters), ras malai (a curdled milk dessert flavored with saffron), and of course the crown jewel of Indian culinary delights, butter paneer!

3. The best way, by far, to visit any Indian city market is in a three-wheeled auto-rickshaw, colloquially known as a "tuk-tuk."

4. Most importantly, to truly experience India, one must become part of the Indian community. Though this seems like a long-term investment, here, a cup of "chai" suffices as an innate rite of passage into people's homes, lives, and hearts. The people of India have taught me the beauty of taking time for others, even people who I may only meet for a moment. These people are not just passersby. They are part of my community, part of my life.

This special land may never "fit" into my western mindset, and to be honest, I hope that it never does. I love India the way that it is. I love caring about people more than a clock. I love taking time to drink chai (a spiced, creamy Assam tea) with my Indian community of friends; and most of all, I am overcome with a love for the generous hospitality of a culture that I have come to love and respect, and by which I feel so supremely honored.

To be sure, India is a land of great contrast. How is it that in this land of palaces, princes, and maharajas (Hindi for "Kings"), there is also some of the greatest human need that I have ever seen? When walking through the streets of Jaipur, it is common to see some of the finest architecture on earth. Across the street from billion-dollar palaces, there are children striving to survive. The questions seem daunting as I wonder, "What in the world happened?" In this land of great love, there is great sorrow. As Amanda and I have traveled throughout the world serving the hurting, we have seen a common denominator throughout humanity.

The poor and hurting are always among us.

From the street-children running towards vehicles with outstretched hands, hoping for a rupee, to the hardened members of Salvadoran gangs, great need seems to be everywhere.

This juxtaposition of opulent and needy society is not limited to the "developing world." Walking outside in the United States and opening one's eyes will reveal similar needs. Children, hungry for love, acceptance, and truth permeate our society. Even in the most developed of all nations, need lingers. The contrast between the beautiful and the desolate can be overwhelming. How are we to make a difference in a world that seems so hopeless and so dark? How can we put the *whole world* into the "Fix-it" box?

The truth is that we do live in a broken world. We are in desperate need of Christ's "Fix-it" box. The answer to the question of the hour seems on the surface, relatively simple. It seems too easy, but it is true nonetheless. The Bible explains that the only way to impact our world is through love, specifically, Christ's love through our lives.

The Love of Christ [For me]

To fully realize a Biblical understanding of the terribly overused word "love," a study of the book of 1 John is necessary. The book is relatively short, and I challenge you now, before you continue this chapter, take some time and read through I John. Pay close attention to chapters three and four, as they are most applicable to answering the question raised in the previous section.

16 We know what real love is because Jesus gave up His life for us... (1 John 3:16)

In this scripture, we see that the love that is commanded of us over and over again throughout the book of 1 John, is not a humanized, self-gratifying, self-seeking love. This love is selfless. The love that God put on display for humanity through Christ giving His life on Calvary is the example of what real, honest, and true love actually is.

I am continually amazed by the fact that God would give Himself for me. Think about this. This is the difference between Christianity and all other world religions. In Christianity, God selflessly gave His life in love for us. God of the universe, all powerful, all mighty, gave himself for *my* justification? This is simply an amazing thought. He *valued* me. Not only did He show true love through sacrifice, but in 1 John 1:9, Christ expresses a desire for restoration and forgiveness!

But if we confess our sins to Him, He is faithful and just to forgive us our sins and cleanse us from all wickedness – 1 John 1:9

This is true, selfless love. Not only did Christ give His life for us, but He also requires no guilt for past mistakes that we have made. He offers cleansing.

Ponder that. He offers cleansing.

The Love of Christ [Through me...For others]

We must return to the question at hand.

"How are we to make a difference in a world that seems so hopeless and so dark?"

7 Dear friends, I am not writing a new

commandment for you; rather it is an old one you have had from the very beginning. This old commandment—to love one another—is the same message you heard before. 8 Yet it is also new. Jesus lived the truth of this commandment, and you also are living it. For the darkness is disappearing, and the true light is already shining. – 1 John 2:7-8 (NLT)

Here, we see that John is expressing a truth that literally shakes my understanding of what it means to love those around me. To sum up the above scripture, I like to use the following statement:

Love is the medium by which the light of the Gospel travels.

This true, unabashed, selfless love for others brings about the Light of Christ into the darkest places on the planet. I may not have the money, resources, or the ability to change people's cirmumstances; however, I have the capacity to love. In Christ, I am able to spread love everywhere I go. Interestingly, in one my favorite passages of scripture, John expresses this truth in staggering words:

11 Dear friends, since God loved us that much, we surely ought to love each other. 12 No one has ever seen God. But if we love each other, God lives in us, and his love is brought to full expression in us. – 1 John 4:11-12 (NLT)

Wow! When we love one another, God's love is brought to *FULL EXPRESSION.* The same love that drove our Infinite Creator to step out of Heaven and onto the earth in order to heal the sick, touch and cleanse the leprous, and to give His life for our sake; is brought into expression when I love others.

That means, that the mountain-moving, life-giving, soul-restoring power of Christ is present when I love someone as Christ has loved me.

I love the implication of this scripture. I do not have to be the most talented singer, the most gifted preacher, or even rich and famous to make a difference in the world for Jesus Christ. The implication is that if I follow His example of selflessly serving and loving those around me, the Gospel will advance.

Responsibility

It is interesting to me that often when I find myself with an opportunity to love those around me, it is quite inconvenient. At first it may seem surprising, but inconvenience is foundational to love. How could I ever express true love if it were convenient?

It would not have the same power. Stopping my life, my routine, and my schedule shouts to others that they are more important to me than I am. In fact, I would go as far as saying that without inconvenience, it is nearly impossible to show love. Think about it. Birthday presents are special, not because of an object, but because someone stopped their life, paid attention to me enough to know what I like, and then took a trip to the store to buy the present. That is why it is so much more fun to open a present than to open an envelope. (I do like gift cards and cash, but they are not the same as an actual gift.)

That being said, Christ-like acts of love are seldom at convenient moments. Taking time to console a friend who is going through something difficult takes time. Spending the afternoon with someone who is lonely takes time. It is not convenient. However, sharing the love of Christ is the cornerstone of our God-given purpose of living.

The only way to bring light into the darkness of the world around us is through love (1 John 2:7-8)!

While Amanda and I were in India, my parents came for a weekend visit. My father was working in Dubai and had the opportunity to fly in for just two days. During the forty-eight hours that they visited the cultural mosaic of Jaipur, we talked, laughed, embraced history, and even rode elephants! This exploration overload left us somewhat tired!

One evening, my mom requested," Jacob, show us your neighborhood. Let's take a quick walk around the block, and then we can come home and rest."

As we left the apartment, we stopped at a local store to buy a soda. I introduced the shopkeeper (who I frequent and to whom I enjoy talking) to my parents. In an instant, the entire agenda for our evening was pulverized. My friend, the shopkeeper, quickly invited us to be his guests for chai. The entire family stopped their activity. My friend's wife stopped cooking dinner, he left the shop with an attendant, and his brother put everything else on hold to come and meet my family. Together for about an hour, we talked (in broken Hindi-English), shared with one another, and enjoyed fellowship.

At the moment of the invitation, we could have made excuses as to why we could not take time to have chai, and we could have passed on this opportunity. However, I am certain that we would have missed the Lord's opportunity to encourage a special family. Often we compartmentalize what constitutes God's love. Preaching, praying, giving, and acts of service are all ways to share God's love; but sitting with a family, enjoying time with others, and sharing life together is also ministry.

So Chai time can change the world?

Not exactly…but yes. Sometimes, sharing the love of Christ is a simple act of relationship. Other times, sharing His love takes selfless action. There are times when we can love others by simply being with them. At other moments, we are called to pack our bags, head across the sea (or even across the street), and proclaim the Gospel with our lives, actions, and words.

Across the globe, from the US to Asia, there are incredible needs. Whether the need is a friendly conversation, desperately needed medical care, or even basic needs of nutrition, meeting these needs in Christ's name jubilantly expresses the love of the Father.

Our first response when faced with a need of any kind is usually, "That's terrible! I wish that I could do something about it." I am convinced that the scriptures speak very clearly to this sentiment.

17 If someone has enough money to live well and sees a brother or sister in need but shows no compassion—how can God's love be in that person?

18 Dear children, let's not merely say that we love each other; let us show the truth by our actions. – 1 John 3:17-18

17 Remember, it is sin to know what you ought to do and then not do it. – James 4:17

The scriptures above firmly express the following:

The *ability* to act [or respond to a need] is the *responsibility* to act [or respond to a need].

So many times, we think that meeting someone's

need is beyond us. Truth be told, in our own strength, we are totally inept. We cannot change the difficulties that fill the earth. However, in Christ, we are more than conquerors. When we love in Christ, we walk in His strength because His love is brought to full expression (1 John 4:12). It is really all about His love reaching the world.

But will it make a difference?

Absolutely.

I have watched the Lord restore broken hearts all over the world. From children, broken by gang violence, to men, at their wits end looking for work, I have watched the Lord restore hearts, minds, and lives. As we share Christ's love, one person at a time, light slowly overshadows darkness (I John 2:7-8).

Each of us is equipped to bring light into this dark world. It may take time, effort, and sometimes, it is downright difficult. In fact, when Amanda and I moved across the world in order to serve with King's Castle in El Salvador, or now as we travel with Healthcare Ministries in various countries, it is never easy to leave home. Leaving behind family, friends, and security is difficult. However, serving the Lord has been the most incredible journey that I could have ever imagined. Every time that I am called to put desires and dreams, or just life, on hold in order to share Christ's love with someone, I am amazed at the incredible blessing that I get to live out.

When Jesus said, "It is better to give than to receive," He meant it! Some of the best experiences in my life have been the result of inconvenient decisions. Don't let inconvenience keep you from fulfilling the awesome privileged life that God has called you to! He calls us to love others. In return we experience the full expression of the love of Christin.   We see His restoring power work throughout humanity, and little by little, we see light overpower darkness as the Father touches life after life in His "Fix-it" box.

Reflection Questions

Take a few minutes and think about the following questions. Stop reading, and have a Holy moment with the Father. Allow Him to speak to your heart, Father to son (or daughter). Then, spend a few minutes sharing your heart with the Father.

1. Have I ever experienced the love of the Father? If so, take a moment and enjoy Christ's love. If not, the invitation to experience the love of the Father is here. Simply ask for the Father to share His love and peace with you.

2. Have I been sharing Christ's love with those around me?

3. Have I taken time away from my own activities to enjoy time with the people around me?

Conclusion

Identity Found

The prison door slammed shut, and I stepped back into the fierce Salvadoran sun. The beads of sweat formed almost instantly on brow, but the heat was barely noticeable. My mind swam with thoughts of the young men that I had just encountered. Their tattooed faces consumed my thoughts. Incredibly, during our short time in the youth prison, two of the boys made a decision to follow Christ. They decided, in essence, to put their lives in the "Fix-it" box.

I have often wondered about those boys. A local pastor frequently visits the youth in this prison, and I pray that he is able to continue to instruct these young men in the ways of Christ, as they allow the Father's love to reshape their understanding of life.

All afternoon and into the evening, I thought of the boys in the prison. The situation in El Salvador seems bleak. What about the other thousands of young men and women that are destroyed by the senseless cycle of gang violence continually on the street?

With the same question in my heart, I woke up the next morning. That day, I was to meet one of our outreach teams in one of our church's zones in San Salvador. I drove carefully into the gang-infested community and listened for the booming sound system of the King's Castle evangelism team. Instantly, I recognized the sounds of a Castle program. I could hear clowns inviting children to the program and kids laughing and playing. The sound was pure joy.

After parking my car, I walked toward the basketball court where a group of children crowded in to see a skit that the team was presenting.

I smiled. "What a wonderful way to spend the afternoon," I thought.

I lifted my eyes and a black colored streak caught my eye. There, on the wall under the basketball goal was the graffiti marking this territory as property of one of El Salvador's infamous street gangs. My heart fell as I looked at the precious children at the program and contrasted the joyous moment with what I had seen in the prison the previous day.

At first my heart was heavy, but then I realized that this was what sharing Christ was all about. These children needed the light of Christ in their lives. They needed to hear about the love of the Father who carefully restores our hearts, minds, and souls when we place our lives in His "Fix-it" box.

As the program came to a close, I was filled with great and unspeakable joy. Dozens of children came forward to participate in special times of prayer to allow Jesus to touch and heal their lives. I watched as the loving hand of Christ repaired the sorrow, the hurt, and the loneliness of the children. In place of broken and destroyed lives, I watched as Christ carefully and intentionally restored the hearts of these children and gave them beautiful, lasting hope. Even in the most horrific places, Christ's "Fix-it" box was readily available.

Just as Christ's love and acceptance was available for the children, it is also available today. It doesn't matter if you are in the middle of a gangland basketball court, alone in your home, or in a corporate office on Wall Street, the power of Christ to restore our lives is available.

Legacy

Years after the "Fix-it" box was retired from use, my father, brother, and I still smile about it. We may even suggest putting a radiator, a golf club, or some other damaged item in the "Fix-it" box. However, recently I was surprised to find out that the "Fix-it" box is not "out of service." It is fully operational, and to my surprise, the business has expanded!

My nephew Riley is one of the brightest children

I have ever met. He is articulate, intelligent, and creative. (I think I sound like a doting uncle.) I was pleasantly surprised to find out one afternoon that he too, is familiar with the concept of the "Fix-it" box. My brother, following in the footsteps of my father, instinctively instituted the "Fix-it" box for Riley's injured toys. From broken "Thomas the Train" cars to Star Wars figurines, my brother now cares for Riley's broken treasures.

I love the idea that important practices are passed on to the next generation. The idea of the "Fix-it" box was so important to my brother and I when we were children. It is only natural that my brother would do the same for Riley. Spiritually, this concept is also true. As Christ delicately restores our life we in turn, must share this "Good News" with others. Christ's loving restoration of our lives, dreams, and even love are not ours to hold on to. So many people are in need of

Christ's "Fix-it" box. This precious gift is meant to be passed on to all we meet.

At first it may seem difficult, but one of the best things about knowing Christ, is sharing His unfathomable love with others. It is so beautiful to watch the Lord restore. If you are reading this book and have friends, family, or coworkers that have not experienced the love of Christ, I pray that you will take the opportunity to share with them the power of Christ's restoration in our lives.

The "Fix-it" box of the Father is not meant to be hidden. Let's share it with the next generation.

A few days ago, Amanda and I found out that we are expecting our first child. It is with great anticipation and expectation that I am preparing for fatherhood. I do not know what awaits as this marvelous journey begins, but there is one thing I know. Our child will definitely have a "Fix-it" box.

ACKNOWLEDGMENTS

Amanda – Thank you for teaching me to step out in faith. I would not be who I am without you. I love you more today than I did yesterday. I am so blessed to have the most incredible wife. I love how we serve the Lord together, side-by-side, like Aquila and Priscilla.

Pop – Thank you for teaching me to be steadfast. Thank you for showing me what the Love of God the Father actually looks like. I love and respect you more than words can express.

Mom – Thank you for teaching me to love learning about Christ. Thank you for teaching me how to pray. I know that in many ways this book is an extension of the love for reading and learning about Christ that we share together. I love you so much.

Matthew – Thank you for believing in me and supporting me in everything I have ever done, from "Hot-Wheelies" to moving to the mission field. Love you bro!

GiGi – Grandmother, thank you so much for all of your love and support over the years. Amanda and I love you dearly, and you have blessed our lives immeasurably! We always look forward to coffee time with GiGi!

Meco – Thank you for teaching me that "Ministry is people." This has been a foundational truth in my life and ministry. You have been more of an example and friend to me than you could ever imagine.

Brother Gary and Mrs. Karen – Thank you for teaching me to listen to the voice of the Lord. Thank you for teaching me to love people with compassion. Thank you for teaching me to share with others life-on-life.

Brother Don – Thank you for teaching me to dream big for the Kingdom of God and to have vision. Your heart and passion for the lost is absolutely contagious. "Raising the dead, that's where it's at. Everything else is just fluff." Brother Don – Summer 2011

Brother Rene – Thank you for faithfully teaching the Word. I remember praying with you to accept Christ when I was five, praying to be commissioned to the mission field when I was twenty-three, and praying together with my wife when we were married in 2010.

Caleb – Thank you for your long-time friendship! Thank you for taking the time to make this book come alive through intricate yet stunning graphics work. You are truly talented my friend!

Angel – Thank you so much for your work in proofreading and editing this book! Your time and effort on this project were an incredible blessing!

ABOUT THE AUTHOR

After graduating from nursing school, Jacob and Amanda Noel served in El Salvador, Central America with King's Castle Ministries. There, they ministered as college and career pastors and directed the King's Castle summer internship program.

In 2012, Jacob and Amanda transitioned to begin working with Healthcare Ministries. Now, based in the United States, they travel worldwide to bring hope to the hurting through health teaching and compassionate care.

Jacob and Amanda live in New Orleans, Louisiana, where Jacob is attending LSU School of Medicine.

Made in the USA
Middletown, DE
04 October 2016